A Gift For:

_____

From:

_____

Published in Nashville, Tennessee, by Thomas Nelson, Inc.

Unless otherwise indicated, Scripture quotations used in this book are from The Holy Bible,
New Century Version (NCV), copyright © 1987, 1988, 1991 by Word Publishing, Dallas, Texas, 75039.
Used by permission.

Scripture quotations marked NKJV are from The New King James Version.
Copyright © 1979, 1980, 1982. Thomas Nelson, Inc.

Scripture quotations marked NIV from the Holy Bible, New International Version®.
Copyright © 1973, 1978, 1984 by International Bible Society.
Used by permission of Zondervan Publishing House. All rights reserved.

Scripture quotations marked NLT are taken from the Holy Bible, New Living Translation,
copyright © 1996. Used by permission of Tyndale House Publishers, Inc., Wheaton, Illinois 60189.
All rights reserved.

Cover Designed by Susan Browne
Interior Designed by Greg Jackson, Thinkpen Design, LLC

ISBN 10: 1-59145-568-5
ISBN 13: 978-1-59145-568-4

Printed in the United States of America
07 08 09 00 HCI 4 3 2 1

FOLLOW
YOUR DREAMS

Wisdom & Inspiration for
GRADUATES

THOMAS NELSON PUBLISHERS
Since 1798

Table of Contents

Dreams Are a Gift from God 09
Take a Risk *Shane Werlinger* 11
Stop and Listen 16
Follow Your Heart *Margaret Lang* 19
Big Dreams 24
Sara's Tea Table *Elece Hollis* 27
God's Promises for Dreaming Big 32

Dreams Give Life Purpose 35
Smiley *Karen Majoris Garrison* 37
Dreamers Who Do 46
A Dream Fulfilled *Jan Madden* 48
Not in Vain *Emily Dickinson* 52
God's Promises of Purpose 53

Dreams Must Overcome Obstacles 55
More Than a Grasshopper *Margaret Lang* 57
Wildflowers *Kitty Chappell* 64
Carpe Diem *Rachel Stewart as told to Teena M. Stewart* 68

Lifting Weights 74

God's Promises for Overcoming Challenges 75

Dreams Must Be Nourished 77

The Place to Be *Melinda Borum as told to Jessica Inman* 79

Don't Go It Alone 86

The Time Between *Sharon Hinck* 89

Prayers to Travel By 96

The Love Letter *Elece Hollis* 99

God's Promises for Nurturing Dreams 104

Dreams Require Work 107

Mr. Goodwrench *Glenn A. Hascall* 109

Be Strong! 112

You Da Man *Nanette Thorsen-Snipes* 114

Go for the Gold 120

God's Promises for Perseverance 121

Dreams Determine Our Tomorrows 123

A Teacher at Last *Eugene Edwards as told
    to Gloria Cassity Stargel* 125

Good Days Ahead 132

Faith for Tomorrow *Thomas Curtis Clark* 133

Lights *Jessica Inman* 135

God's Promises for Bright Tomorrows............... 141

Dreams Will Grow and Change 143

Major Disappointment *Kate Frezon as told to Peggy Frezon* .. 145

You Never Know 150

When Visions Grow 155

God's Promises for Growing Dreams................ 159

Acknowledgments................................ 160

Yes, God made all things,
and everything continues
through him and for him.

ROMANS 11:36A

DREAMS ARE A GIFT FROM GOD

We all have dreams. They whisper to us in the middle of the mundane, calling our attention above studying or running or watching TV.

Our dreams are a part of us, born out of our personalities, hopes, and desires. They were knit inside us as God thoughtfully and carefully knit us together. Dreams and the sense of purpose they bring are one of God's best gifts. They make us feel truly alive and give meaning to the future. Best of all, they inspire us to walk more closely with the One who gave us our dreams.

When God plants a dream in your heart, enjoy it—and give thanks to Him for what the days ahead will bring.

We all have big
changes in our lives
that are more or less
a second chance.

HARRISON FORD

Take a Risk

SHANE WERLINGER

As I pulled up to the job site, I blew my breath out slowly. *I don't know how much longer I can do this*, I groaned inwardly. I popped the trunk and wandered back to grab my tools. I cinched the tool belt around my waist, the weight of the pouch an anchor to my spirits. The workday of a siding installer was about to begin.

I used to love construction. But ever since I fell off a ladder on the jobsite, shattering my left ankle along with my fearlessness, things just hadn't been the same. Whispers of fear filled my mind every time I stepped onto a ladder, and plus the work just wasn't very exciting anymore. The effort of fighting my anxieties and trying to muster some enthusiasm was wearing me down.

Later that evening I sat at the dinner table with my wife, Sandy, and inhaled the scrumptious feast she'd made. But for some reason, the pork chops and scalloped potatoes didn't have their usual effect on me. Sandy's cooking could always chase away the vestiges of a bad day, but the cloud that had been looming over me all day continued to linger.

"Honey," I started, languidly cutting into a pork chop, "I'm starting to dread going into work every morning and I don't know what to do."

She looked at me thoughtfully for a moment and then asked the question that changed my life.

"Have you ever thought that maybe construction isn't for you?"

I put my fork down and looked into her eyes to see if she was joking. I had been doing some form of construction since I was a teenager, and I'd planned to keep at it until I retired. It's true I wasn't happy in my current work situation, but leave construction altogether? The thought had never entered my mind.

I shook my head no and reached for the salt. "What else would I do? I left college to work in construction. I think I'm a little old to start something new, don't you?"

"You're only twenty-seven. You can do anything you want to. If you want to stay in construction, I'm fine with that, but do you really want to hate going to work every day for the rest of your life? It's up to you. Whatever you want to do, I'm behind you."

"Well, I'll think about it, sweetheart."

As we kept eating, her question sat on my lap. How

could construction not be for me? I had been working on people's houses for years. I couldn't even envision what else I would do if I didn't do construction. Still . . . did I want to spend the rest of my life dreading my days on the jobsite?

I went back to work, of course. The days kept dragging on, Sandy's question running laps through my mind all the while. What other jobs could I do? What kind of job did I want? The more I searched my soul, the more I knew I had to act, and I started looking into going back to school. But what would I study?

I weighed all my options, and after a while one of them grew brighter and brighter until I knew God had led me to it. Soon after, I applied at a technical school to enroll in their network administration program—I wanted to be a computer tech. Computers were everywhere, and I knew that there would always be a need for someone to make sure they were up and running. Plus, I'd always had computer-geek tendencies. So I started classes that January and went to school for fifteen months straight, four nights a week, five hours a night.

Just because I was going to school didn't mean the bills stopped rolling in. I still had to work forty-plus hours a week. Between work, school, and homework, I didn't have a lot of spare time, and there were moments when I thought about throwing in the towel. But the light at the end of the tunnel was getting brighter, and hope kept rekindling that my goal would be met. Finally, I graduated in March with honors.

I stood in front of the full-length mirror adjusting my tie, getting ready to step into the auditorium for the graduation ceremony. As I pulled the gown over my head, I reflected on the changes that had already occurred since starting school.

After eleven months of school and getting my certification, I was able to make the transition to my new career. The previous November, I'd landed a position on a computer helpdesk. I had gotten out of the elements and into an office. Now I was about to walk across the stage and make it all official.

I turned from the mirror to pose for Sandy. It had been almost ten years since I wore a cap and gown.

"So, how do I look?" I asked.

"Like a scholar," Sandy said, adjusting my honor ropes. "I can't believe this is all about to be over. I thought it would never end."

"I know. It's hard to believe."

"Well, you better get going," she said, planting a kiss on my cheek. "I'm so proud of you." With that, she left for the auditorium.

I got in line with my classmates and we were herded in to the auditorium. I sat in my seat as each speaker gave their speech. I had been waiting for this moment for over a year. Finally they called my name. I floated across that stage as I shook the hand of the instructors and received my certification.

Things have only gotten better since then. I have moved up in my field, and God has provided for us enough that my wife can stay home with our daughter, which had always been a goal for our family. When I look back now, I see God's hand in everything. He put the question in Sandy's heart, that one little question that changed our lives—"Do you really want to hate going to work every day?" One little question called me out of my comfort zone and made our dreams come true. ∎

I am guiding you in the way of wisdom,
and I am leading you on the right path. Nothing
will hold you back; you will not be overwhelmed.

PROVERBS 4:11–12

Stop and Listen

The months leading up to graduation are a busy time in our lives—ceremonies, final exams and projects, and plenty of parties. Amid all the frenetic activity, it's easy to get caught up in details and miss the big picture.

To get some direction and a sense of purpose and peace, it's not a bad idea to take a little time out. Work a quiet minute into your busy schedule. Go to a park to walk and pray. Spend half an hour with your Bible and a journal in a tucked-away corner of your school. Dream dreams for the future and express gratitude for the past and present.

Don't let this exciting time in your life pass by in a flurry of stress and activity. Take a minute to listen to the dreams God wants to place in your heart. ■

*You keep your
loving promise and
lead the people
you have saved.*

EXODUS 15:13A

As we trust God to give us
wisdom for today's decisions,
He will lead us a step at a time
into what He wants us
to be doing in the future.

THEODORE EPP

Follow Your Heart

MARGARET LANG

From the time Anna was five years old, all she ever wanted to do was "chat" with her friend Alicia. The girls regularly played in the sand pile together, digging long trenches with plastic shovels and building sand castles. Even though Alicia was deaf from cerebral palsy and Anna wasn't, the two friends communicated perfectly with each other—not with words the way other kids do, but with their hands.

When Alicia moved across town, Anna missed her and the reciprocal hand game. Normal talk with other kids seemed boring in comparison.

"I just want to chat with Alicia," Anna complained to Jesus on her knees beside her bed.

As she grew older, that thought never went away. She wrote her thoughts to the Lord and kept praying about her desire to communicate with Alicia, and one day He answered. His loving presence helped fill the loneliness in her life and He encouraged her to follow her heart. Anna knew that meant learning sign language. But how?

Seemingly out of nowhere, a sign language interpreter came to teach classes at Anna's small church. Anna jumped right in and soon her fingers danced out the words of the worship songs. She discovered that signing came naturally to her.

No matter how hard she practiced her lessons, Anna knew something was missing. "If only Alicia still lived next door. I really want to see her," Anna said to her mom. "I could sign with her and become really good so that I could help other deaf people."

So Anna's mom found a way to contact Alicia, and expectantly, they drove the many miles to her house.

"You've grown up, Alicia," signed Anna as she hugged her friend.

"So have you, Anna," Alicia signed back with a big smile.

Like the subjects of a silent animated film, the teen girls sat down on the sofa and eagerly shared their hearts. Alicia signed the plots of her favorite movies. And Anna signed about her favorite subject, the Lord. "You're special to Jesus," she said to Alicia, touching her palms to symbolize the nails in His hands.

Because she lived so far away, Anna didn't get to see Alicia very much after that. She kept journaling her thoughts and feelings, and the impression she felt from the Lord was always the same: "I love your heart, Anna. Just follow it."

Anna did. When it came time to choose a college, she picked one that offered courses in American Sign Language. In her first week of school, she bumped right into Alicia on the sidewalk. "What a surprise! I didn't know we both chose the same college," she signed.

The two friends got together every day, between classes, at the cafeteria, anytime and anyplace. They also enjoyed deaf events together, especially pizza night. They ate and signed non-stop. Practice made perfect, and soon signing became more natural for Anna than speaking.

Anna easily received her certification in sign language interpreting and a community college immediately hired her part-time. For several years, she interpreted a few classes, until she began to desire more—much more.

"It would be nice, Lord, if I could find a full-time job," Anna wrote in her journal. "But without a degree, that might be difficult."

"Follow your heart and trust Me," came His faithful reply.

Right at that time, a neighbor told Anna about a full-time job in a school system. Anna jumped at the opportunity. When the director tested Anna, she found her skill level much higher than her academic level would indicate. She hired her on the spot—waiving the required degree. "We've never done this for anyone before. We're also willing to pay for your license and help you earn your degree."

Anna was dumbfounded by the favor. A full-time job, a license, and a degree opportunity. How did it all happen?

Then it dawned on her. Because she had followed the Lord with all her heart, He had guided her steps and encouraged her to follow her dreams. And her God-given gifting made a way for her.

She told Alicia, "I'm happy and I thank God—and you."

"Why, Anna?"

"Years ago in the sand pile, you were my inspiration." As Anna signed the heartfelt words to her longtime friend, her fingers fanned out and pointed upward towards heaven, a gesture of her gratefulness. ∎

Take delight in the LORD,
and he will give you
your heart's desires.

PSALM 37:4 NLT

Big Dreams

The next time you're feeling a little shaky about the dreams God has for you, remember these heroes who followed their God-given dreams:

- *Abraham.* He had a promise from God to make him a great nation, and he held onto that dream with a tenacity that would make him an icon of faith for ages to come.

- *Moses.* Moses dreamed of freedom for his people, and he allowed God to use him to lead Israel out of the bondage of Egypt.

- *David.* David wanted to see the giant defeated and God's name vindicated, so much so that he was willing to fight Goliath himself—and he won.

• *Nehemiah.* When he heard that the wall of his beloved city had been destroyed, he dreamed of seeing it restored. He prayed and traveled and organized and fought off the opposition, and the wall was rebuilt.

Take heart: When God gives you something to do, He'll be beside you every step of the way, and you're in for the adventure of your life. ∎

> *The beautiful thing about*
> *this adventure called faith*
> *is that we can count on Him*
> *never to lead us astray.*
> Charles R. Swindoll

The "least of my brethren"
are the hungry and the lonely,
not only for food, but for the Word
of God; the thirsty and the ignorant
not only for water, but also for
knowledge, peace, truth,
justice, and love.

MOTHER TERESA

Sara's Tea Table

ELECE HOLLIS

Sara invited me to come visit her that afternoon. She had cleared a spot in the squalor of her parents' apartment, spreading a small square of silky cloth—a former scarf, on closer inspection—across a rickety coffee table. She had decorated the spot with her most prized possessions: a pocket New Testament, a red plastic comb, a tiny beaded trinket, and a faded silk flower, one on each corner of the scarf.

I never quite envisioned myself here—"here" meaning a tiny, filthy apartment in my native United States. Ever since I was twelve, I just knew the wind would take me far away to Asia, Africa, or South America. I would be a missionary, the "mother" of an orphanage. I would waltz through a cobbled courtyard, patting adoring little girls on the head, my voice like music to their love-starved ears. They would lean against my freshly pressed skirts and look up at me with trusting eyes from sweet, clean faces, brimming with obvious affection and gratitude.

This was a deep dream, one I heartily pursued throughout my teen years. When I heard of a woman who ran an orphanage in Brazil, I wrote and offered my services. I applied for a passport and started packing. I was going!

But then came the letter saying, "Do not come. There are problems which I cannot explain at this time. I must return to the States. Do not come."

And so I went instead to work in Washington State on an Indian reservation. There I found the love-starved children I'd always envisioned—and physically starved children as well. I found many problems that I could not have foreseen, problems not at all confined to Brazilian orphanages.

There were little faces, but few were clean or sweet. Many were neglected, sickly, abused, and mistrustful. And some were very angry. Here I found real pain and suffering, poverty and ignorance, right in my home country. I also found myself empty-handed and ignorant of how to help.

How could I help Sara, a half-starved nine-year-old girl who lived in a filthy hovel with her abusive, alcoholic parents? A pat on the head and a simplistic Sunday school song wouldn't give her clothes to wear, decent food to eat, a clean bed to sleep in, a chance to learn to read and write, or a minute's peace from hardship.

At Sara's tea table I was the honored guest. She presented me with a cup of water. My heart ached for her, a precious little person trapped in a harsh world. I sat and sipped my water and fought back tears. Could I even fathom the cruel realities of her life?

My whole life had been idyllic and placid. I had never endured one day of hunger. I had never been mistreated or neglected. I had been nurtured and tenderly cared for since birth.

Sara had never once sat on her daddy's lap to be read a story. She had never been dressed in a starched and ruffled dress, ribbons tied in her hair, to be given a birthday party complete with balloons, favors, and a big chocolate cake. There was never anyone to "ooh" and "ah" over her saying her ABC's or applaude her singing in a Christmas pageant.

Never had she been taken by her grandpa to swing and play in the park or climb up on a stool and sip a soda at the local drugstore. She had not known any of the carefree, safe, normal childhood experiences. She had suffered all her life in poverty and degradation—yet she had hope.

There it was on our makeshift tea table: her Bible, her only hope, her chance in life for deliverance and happiness. I could assure her of that. She couldn't read it, but I could help her know what it said: that Somebody loved her. God, a kind Father—one who would never abuse her, who would not scream at her, beat her, or lie drunk on the floor—loved her. He loved *her*, Sara.

At the end of that summer, I went home and back to college, my vision of the world seriously altered. I had begun to grow up, for I had experienced my own powerlessness. I had realized that the world ranged far beyond my borders. There were many problems I could not understand. My childhood visions of what it would be like to serve as a missionary were simply not going to happen; they were going to have to adapt. I grieved for that dream lost.

Yet, I had a new dream. God had shown me something: Jesus was the only answer for people like Sara. My new dream was to bring His love into the darkest places in the hurting world I'd just discovered.

As I went back to classes, I felt God tucking this dream into my heart. I knew I would have to depend on Him to make it a reality. But I also knew He would help me, because I knew this dream was from Him. ■

*So go and make followers of all
people in the world. Baptize them
in the name of the Father and the Son
and the Holy Spirit. Teach them to obey
everything that I have taught you,
and I will be with you always, even
until the end of this age.*

Matthew 28:19–20

God's Promises for Dreaming Big

*The Lord will always lead you. He will satisfy your needs
in dry lands and give strength to your bones. You will be like a
garden that has much water, like a spring that never runs dry.*

ISAIAH 58:11

*The Lord will fulfill his purpose for me;
your love, O LORD, endures forever—
do not abandon the works of your hands.*

PSALM 138:8 NIV

*God began doing a good work in you, and I am sure he will
continue it until it is finished when Jesus Christ comes again.*

PHILIPPIANS 1:6

*And God is able to make all grace abound toward you,
that you, always having all sufficiency in all things,
may have an abundance for every good work.*

2 CORINTHIANS 9:8 NKJV

But as it is written in the Scriptures:
"No one has ever seen this, and no one
has ever heard about it. No one
has ever imagined what God has prepared
for those who love him."

1 CORINTHIANS 2:9

Do not change yourselves to be like
the people of this world, but be changed
within by a new way of thinking. Then you
will be able to decide what God wants for you;
you will know what is good and pleasing
to him and what is perfect.

ROMANS 12:2

*God has made us what we are.
In Christ Jesus, God made us to do
good works, which God planned in
advance for us to live our lives doing.*

EPHESIANS 2:10

DREAMS GIVE LIFE PURPOSE

What is life without goals to work toward? Our days feel so much richer when we believe they're taking us directly, intentionally toward better ones.

And the best goals of all are the ones that bring us closer to our dreams, the dreams instilled in us by our wise and wonderful God. The dreams He gives us are the most thrilling of all, because they meet needs and share grace and show kindness—they do things in keeping with God's great character.

Dreams give us hope. They give us meaningful goals. And they give us a sense that life is about more than ourselves.

I am a little pencil in
the hand of a writing God
who is sending a love
letter to the world.

MOTHER TERESA

Smiley

KAREN MAJORIS GARRISON

Maybe I was a little self-centered. Or maybe I was closer to full-on prima donna. In any case, I was seventeen, and all I wanted to do was graduate—and enhance my final Health Assistant grade. Toward that end, I volunteered at the nearby convalescent center.

For weeks I grumbled to my boyfriend. "I can't believe I'm stuck with tending to old people for free." He agreed. I soon realized that the bright yellow uniforms my classmates and I were required to wear made matters even worse. On our first day at the center, the nurses took one look at our sunshiny apparel and nicknamed us "the yellow birds."

During my days at the center, I complained to the other "yellow birds" about how emptying bedpans, changing soiled linens, and spoon-feeding pureed foods to mumbling mouths were not tasks any teenager should have to do.

A tedious month passed, and then I met Lily. I was given a tray of food and sent to her room. Her bright blue eyes appraised me as I entered, and I quickly became very aware of the kindness behind them.

After talking with her for a few minutes, I realized why I hadn't noticed Lily before, even though I had walked past her room numerous times. Lily, unlike some of the other residents, was soft-spoken and undemanding. From my first day at the geriatric center, I had learned that the staff had their favorite patients. Usually the favored residents stuck out in some charac- teristic way. From joke-tellers to singers, the louder and more rambunctious the patient, the more attention they received. Quiet Lily was all but forgotten.

Something inside of me immediately liked Lily and I even began to enjoy our talks during my visits to her room. It didn't take long to realize that Lily's genuine kindness stemmed from her relationship with God.

"Come here," she smiled to me one rainy afternoon. "Sit down. I have something to show you." She lifted a small photo album and began to turn the pages. "This was my Albert. See him there? Such a handsome man." Her voice softened even more as she pointed to a pretty little girl sitting on top of a fence. "And that was our darling Emmy when she was eight years old."

A drop of wetness splattered on the plastic cover and I quickly turned to Lily. Her eyes were filled with tears. "What is it?" I whispered, covering her hand with my own.

She didn't answer right away, but as she turned the pages I noticed that Emmy was not in any other photographs. "She died from cancer that year," Lily told me. "She'd been in and out of hospitals most of her life, but that year Jesus took her home."

"I'm so sorry," I said, disturbed that God would take away this beautiful woman's daughter. "I don't understand how that could happen to such good people."

"It's okay," she smiled slightly, meeting my eyes. "God has a plan for every life, Karen. We need to open our hearts to Him whether we understand His ways or not. Only then can we find true peace." She turned to the last page. Inside the worn album was one more picture of a middle-aged Lily standing on tiptoes and kissing a clown's cheek.

"That's my Albert," she laughed, recalling happier memories. "After Emmy died, we decided to do something to help the children at the hospitals. We'd been so disturbed by the dismal surroundings while Emmy was hospitalized." Lily went on to explain how Albert decided to become "Smiley the Clown."

"Emmy was always smiling, even in the worst of times. So I scraped together what fabric I could find and sewed this costume for Albert." She clasped her hands in joy. "The children loved it! Every weekend, we'd volunteer at the hospitals to bring smiles and gifts to the children."

"How'd you manage to afford that?" I asked in amazement.

"Well," she grinned, "smiles are free, and the gifts weren't anything fancy." She closed the album and leaned back against her pillows. "Sometimes the local bakers donated goodies, or when we were really hurting for money, we'd take a litter of pups from our farm. The children loved petting them. After Albert died, I noticed how faded and worn the costume was, so I rented one and dressed as Smiley myself; that is . . . until my first heart attack, about ten years ago."

When I left Lily's room that day, I couldn't think of anything but how generous she and Albert had been to children who weren't even their own. I thought about my own life and how I rarely did anything for anyone other than myself.

Graduation day neared, and on my last day of volunteer services at the ward, I hurried to Lily's room. She was asleep, curled into a fetal position from stomach discomfort. I stroked her brow, worrying about who would care for her the way I did. She didn't have any surviving family members, and most of the staff neglected her except for her basic needs, which were met with polite abruptness. At times, I wanted to proclaim Lily's virtues to the staff, but she'd stop me, reminding me that the good things she'd done in life were done without thoughts of self.

"Besides," she would say, "doesn't the good Lord tell us to store our treasures in heaven and not on this earth?"

Lily must've sensed my inner torment above her bed that day as she opened her eyes and touched my hand. "What is it, dear?" she asked, her voice concerned and laced with pain.

"I'll be back in two weeks," I told her, explaining about my high school graduation. "And then I'll visit you every day. I promise."

She sighed and squeezed my fingers. "I can't wait for you to tell me all about it."

Two weeks later to the day, I rushed back to the center, bubbly with excitement and anxious to share with Lily the news of my graduation events. With a bouquet of lilies in my hand, I stepped into her clean, neat, unoccupied room and saw the tidily made bed. As I searched for an answer to Lily's whereabouts, my heart already knew what had happened.

I threw the flowers on the bed and wept.

A nurse gently touched my shoulder. "Were you one of the yellow birds?" she asked. "Is your name Karen?" I nodded and she handed me a gift-wrapped box. "Lily wanted you to have this. We've had it since she died because we didn't know how to get in touch with you."

It was her photo album. Written on the inside cover was the scripture Jeremiah 29:11: "'I know what I am planning for you,' says the Lord. 'I have good plans for you, not plans to hurt you. I will give you hope and a good future.'" I clutched the album to my chest and departed.

Three weeks later, my horrified boyfriend stood before me. "You can't be serious," he said, pacing back and forth. "You look ridiculous."

We were in my bedroom, and as I tried to view myself in the mirror, he blocked my reflection. "You can't be serious," he repeated. "How in the world did you pay for that thing, anyway?"

"God has a plan for me," I answered. "So I spent my graduation money on it."

"Your what?" he exclaimed, shaking his head. "What about our plans? You spent the money that we saved for New York on that?

"Yep," I replied, stringing on my rubber nose. "Life is more about giving than receiving." Knowing Lily had given me a new purpose, a new sense of what was really important.

"This is just great," he muttered, helping me tie the back of the costume. "And what am I supposed to tell someone when they ask me my girlfriend's name? That it's Bozo?"

I looked at my watch. I had better hurry if I wanted to make it on time to the children's hospital. "Nope," I answered, kissing him quickly on the cheek. "Tell them it's Smiley—Smiley the Clown." ■

I tell you the truth, anything you did for even
the least of my people here, you also did for me.

Matthew 25:40

The most important thing is that I complete my mission, the work that the Lord Jesus gave me—to tell people the Good News about God's grace.

ACTS 20:24

This is the true joy
in life, the being used
for a purpose recognized
by yourself as a mighty one.

GEORGE BERNARD SHAW

Dreamers Who Do

When we have dreams and goals to work toward, we're happier, more productive people. When we take steps—when we do things—to achieve something meaningful and purposeful, life is simply more fulfilling and exciting.

And it may not be all in our heads. Studies have long shown that people who volunteer report greater overall health, and some studies suggest that doing things to help others may improve insomnia and boost our immune systems.

So don't just dream—*do*. Let God give you dreams that will help others, and take a step today toward making those dreams happen. ■

People will be rewarded for what they say,
and they will also be rewarded for what they do.

PROVERBS 12:14

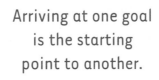

Arriving at one goal
is the starting
point to another.

JOHN DEWEY

A Dream Fulfilled

JAN MADDEN

"Okay, boys and girls, let's work on our ABC's today."

Baby dolls and teddy bears sat in neat little rows on my bed listening attentively to my "professional" seven-year-old voice—except for that Joey. I had sent that little teddy bear to the principal's office more times than I could count.

Turning back to the miniature green chalkboard which Santa had delivered last Christmas, I continued my lesson. My little "students" had to be the smartest in all of middle Tennessee. I taught them almost every day, including summers and weekends.

At the end of both kindergarten and first grade, teachers gave me discarded textbooks and unused workbooks. Mom always pretended to be as excited as I was about those old, dusty books' new residence.

As a twelve-year-old, I somehow talked my sixth grade teacher into letting me teach a handwriting class to a group of fellow students. I gathered my little flock to one side of the classroom and began to help them form their cursive letters correctly. It would seem that I was destined to become a teacher.

But after I graduated from high school, circumstances led me into numerous jobs, none of which related to the field of education, and none of which required more than a high school diploma. I was far away from my dream career as a teacher.

Nonetheless, the dream stayed alive, pulsing in my chest. And one day, I decided to make a change, to take a step toward making my dream come true. I enrolled in college as an Elementary Education major with a Psychology minor. I loved it. However, after two years, tragedy struck my life, and my world tumbled upside down.

My daughter perished in a house fire, and within months after that my marriage ended. I re-enrolled in college and tried to persevere, but soon quit. Life—and grief—had overwhelmed me.

Miraculously, God brought a wonderful Christian man into my life. We married and, over the course of several years, God blessed our marriage with three extraordinary sons.

Soon after our third son's birth, we accepted an opportunity to work in a private Christian boarding school. I worked not as a teacher, but as partner with my husband as dorm dean. I also worked as the school's secretary part time.

Daily I watched men and women of all ages who taught students. They made a lasting impact on lives. They lived out my dream.

That familiar stirring filled my heart like never before.

The president of the school encouraged me to pursue my dream. He made phone calls and even researched a reputable, accredited seminary that offered correspondence courses. The price was affordable, the courses were exciting, and the two years of courses I had already taken could be applied to my course of study. Nothing stood in my way.

Finally, one warm August afternoon, I wore a black cap and gown and shook hands with the seminary's president as he awarded me a Bachelor's degree in Religious Education. Two years later, after some additional courses, I attained certification to teach in a private Christian school.

Dream fulfilled.

For five years, I stood before a classroom full of exciting junior high and high school students. Cherished relationships developed between us, and I saw both amazing progress and devastating failures.

And then our own son began to need special academic attention. My husband and I thought through all our options. And after thinking it over—and over and over again—just before Christmas break, I asked for a meeting with my principle. With a lump in my throat, I explained that I wouldn't be coming back the following school year. I was going to be a home-school mom.

Early one morning, the fire crackled in the fireplace, the house quiet. I was a little despondent. I wasn't sure I was doing the right thing by leaving; I was going to miss the classroom. Was my dream of being a teacher over after five short years?

I whispered prayers and read Scriptures, and finally I fell into a deep peace that I knew was from God. I knew we had made the right decision.

I became even surer in the following months spent helping my son learn and grow. I celebrated his victories, my heart thrilled. I embraced the challenges and reveled even in the hard days. All the while, I thanked God for enabling me to become a teacher just when my son needed it most.

A dream surrendered to God became a dream fulfilled. Maybe I didn't end up exactly where I'd envisioned myself as a seven-year-old playing with dolls, but I ended up exactly where I needed to be. ■

> *Yet who knows whether you have come*
> *to the kingdom for such a time as this?*
> ESTHER 4:14B NKJV

Not in Vain

EMILY DICKINSON

If I can stop one heart from breaking,
I shall not live in vain:
If I can ease one life the aching,
Or cool one pain,
Or help one fainting robin
Unto his nest again,
I shall not live in vain.

Act as if what you do
makes a difference. It does.

WILLIAM JAMES

God's Promises of Purpose

I came to give life—life in all its fullness.

John 10:10b

You did not choose me; I chose you.
And I gave you this work: to go and
produce fruit, fruit that will last.

John 15:16a

The Lord has made everything
for his own purposes.

Proverbs 16:4a nlt

Lead me in the path
of your commands, because
that makes me happy.

Psalm 119:35

*Let us run the race that is
before us and never give up.
We should remove from our lives
anything that would get
in the way and the sin that
so easily holds us back.*

HEBREWS 12:1B

DREAMS MUST OVERCOME OBSTACLES

~~~~~~~~~~~~

World history is full of dreams that came true. What all dreams have in common, though, is that they all had to overcome challenges in order to come to fruition.

In the life cycle of a dream, there is always a point, usually near the beginning, where the dream-follower feels overwhelmed by the challenges that lie ahead. All we can do is keep our heads and tackle the obstacles one at a time, praying for wisdom and support and maintaining faith that things will turn out okay.

When we do that, we get past the first obstacle, and then another and another, gaining momentum and confidence. Sometimes it requires a few steps of faith, steps that are rewarded in the end.

It doesn't matter whether
you're short of money,
people, energy, or time.
What God invites you to do
will always be greater than
the resources you start with.

BRUCE WILKINSON

More Than a Grasshopper

MARGARET LANG

She skillfully lifted my partially paralyzed leg. Behind the privacy curtains I could hear the voices of other people whose lives and bodies had been cut down. I didn't know who they were or if they—or I— would ever be able to walk again. But I desperately wanted to become a physical therapist like the woman who so compassionately worked with me. The trouble was, with my health problems, I wasn't sure how that would ever happen.

Back at home, I sat in my wheelchair by the window, watching neighbor kids running and playing outside. One little boy was too small to pull his bulky red wagon, and it kept veering off onto the grass and tipping over. The other kids left him behind, and he burst into tears. But then his older brother came back, put his arm around the little guy's shoulders, and pulled the wagon for him.

As I watched from the window, I saw myself yoked to my big brother, Jesus, His arm hooked around my shoulders. Together we could surely pull my load. I could walk again—and reach my dream of becoming a physical therapist. I was going to go for it.

Soon I could walk from chair to chair and class to class, only short distances and in a slow, painful gait—but I could walk. If no chair was available, I just sat down on the floor. Sports, of course, were out.

By the time senior year rolled around, all my friends had become the school leaders and athletes. They were like giants to me, able to achieve anything they wanted, and I felt like a lowly grasshopper. I felt limited, lacking the things it would take to reach my dream. But like Joshua and Caleb, I was determined to enter my Promised Land. Somehow.

When I told my friends I planned to study physical therapy in college so that I could teach others how to walk, they just stared at me with a sympathetic look. I could hear their thoughts: "How can you teach others to walk if you can barely walk yourself?"

For the next four years, I wrapped my leg in Ace bandages and did my best to limp across my college campus. Unrelentingly focused on doing well in my classes, I barely felt the pain of the wear and tear to my tendons and ligaments.

There were other obstacles besides my ailing body. "You should become a teacher," my father often nudged, "just like your mother." But I wouldn't budge. It was tough to say no to my dad, my biggest fan and one of my favorite people, but I had to keep after my dream.

Chemistry proved to be a much bigger obstacle than my dad's opinions. I thought taking it in summer school would be the short and easy way to get the needed credits, but suffice it to say that test tubes and chemicals were not my forte. But by the grace of God—and not my chemistry grade—I squeaked into the graduate physical therapy program in the fall.

Unfortunately, the very morning of my first class, my leg and foot took the inopportune moment to swell up like a water balloon and become unbearably painful. I took a shaky breath. I just had to convince my professors—and myself—that I could do the work of a physical therapist.

My boyfriend carried me from my dorm to the classroom and put me down outside the door. For nine years I had waited for this day to cross my Jordan and walk into my first professional physical therapy class. As I limped over the threshold, the professors seemed like giants and I, again, felt like a grasshopper in their sight. But I still believed that with God helping me, I could succeed.

In the following weeks, the swelling went down and my leg and I remained unnoticed—until one afternoon.

"Margaret, why don't you come down and be our subject for demonstration?" said my professor, a lady I had grown to admire and wanted to impress. She was about to prove that her methods of facilitation worked—on me. Only she didn't know I was not the normal test subject.

Tentatively, I approached the treatment table and lay down. I had two legs. Surely she'd use the good one, I thought.

Wrong. She reached for my bad one and began manual stimulation to produce a flexion response at the ankle—which, of course, did not occur because some of my muscle groups were paralyzed.

She paused. I held my breath. She then took more drastic measures and put the ankle into a painful stretch.

My entire leg sprang back out of harm's way like a released rubber band, and she and I looked at one another at an impasse. I was scared—in that anxious moment I wondered if I would get thrown out of the program right there.

"Thank you, Margaret. You may get off the table. Do I have another volunteer?" Whew. No questions. Again the grace of God. I breathed a sigh of relief.

Even more grace appeared when a doctor affiliated with the school privately taught me a new way to walk. Although I still couldn't walk far and the pain remained, the appearance of my gait improved, and I could finally go to class without people asking me why I was limping. I no longer felt so conspicuous walking across campus.

Time went on, and on graduation day I was numb. I couldn't quite believe I'd achieved what I'd set out to achieve all those years ago. It only hit home when the state board issued my license and a rehabilitation center actually hired me.

The week before my first day at work, my cheeks flushed the color of my red hair with excitement and anticipation.

My first patient, a quadriplegic from a diving accident, wanted more than anything to learn to take a few steps. A boy born with cerebral palsy asked me, "Why am I like this, Red?" A good-hearted truck driver who had jackknifed his semi despaired to live at all. To avoid hitting a car full of drunken teens, he had sacrificed himself and was left totally paralyzed on a rotating frame day and night.

As I treated these saints, I didn't feel my own pain at all. And I couldn't answer their inner questions, the "why" questions that haunted them. I was just humbly honored to be allowed to work with people who were going through such difficulties. Those voices I heard long ago behind the treatment room curtains now had faces, personalities, hopes.

My first week at work ended much too fast, and on Saturday, I volunteered to take patients for an outing to see the Blue Angels perform. Afterwards I wheeled them to my tiny apartment, positioning their wheelchairs pedal-to-pedal, and poured lemonade. Yes, moving the heavy equipment with their human cargo caused added pressure to my leg and foot. They painfully swelled up that night, but I didn't care. I had a mission, a purpose.

When my supervisor handed me my first paycheck, I hesitated to take it. "You mean I get paid to do what I love?" I wanted to ask.

In the afterglow of my fulfilled dream, I had forgotten all about getting paid. I saw myself ten years younger with a disabled leg, admiring my own physical therapist. *Can I ever do what she does?* I had wondered, awed.

Just like the boy with the red wagon, Jesus had come along beside me, and we had pulled the load together. And how easy His yoke had been and how light His burden.

I took the check and gave thanks—amazed at God's faithfulness to me. ■

Be strong and of good courage,
do not fear nor be afraid of them;
for the LORD your God, He is
the One who goes with you.
He will not leave you
nor forsake you.

DEUTERONOMY 31:6 NKJV

Wildflowers

KITTY CHAPPELL

Lord, help me to grow as the wildflowers grow
    be it in a meadow or crack in cement—
Despite the terrain, be it good or bad,
    let me know I am there by intent.

Instead of my sadly complaining within
    regarding life's rough terrain,
May my face, too, look upward to You
    through seasons of drought and rain.

Help me to bloom as the wildflowers bloom,
    regardless of where I am placed;
Wherever the spot You plant me, Lord,
    let the air there be sweet with Your grace.

Someday a tired pilgrim may stop to rest
    from carrying his heavy load
And thank my Creator for placing me there
    to brighten that spot in life's road.

The important thing is
to strive towards a goal
which is not immediately visible.
That goal is not the concern
of the mind, but of the spirit.

ANTOINE DE SAINT-EXUPÉRY

God has a great race
for you to run. Under His care,
you'll go where you've never been
and serve in ways you've never
dreamed. But you have to
release your burdens.

MAX LUCADO

Cast your burden on the LORD, And He shall sustain you;
He shall never permit the righteous to be moved.

PSALM 55:22 NKJV

Experience
is not what
happens to a man.
It is what a man
does with what
happens to him.

ALDOUS HUXLEY

Carpe Diem

RACHEL STEWART AS TOLD TO TEENA M. STEWART

This wasn't how it was supposed to be, I brooded as I as settled into life in Colorado. Rather than move with the rest of my family when Dad accepted a new job, I chose to remain behind at the University of Northern Colorado. It had been a tough decision, and I made it a point to rib my parents about "abandoning" me every chance I got. But I knew it was the right thing to do—transferring schools would have been difficult, and since I would have had to start over on many of my credits, I probably wouldn't have graduated on time.

Now I pinched myself in disbelief as I prepared for my graduation. I couldn't wait to see my family. "They're having the graduation ceremony outdoors, rain or shine," I told them. I thought of my high school graduation and how we'd all baked in the Colorado sun on metal bleachers. During the ceremony, my dad had mistakenly videotaped the wrong girl in cap and gown—lining up for the procession, waving to the stands, walking down the aisle. Only when they called my name to receive my diploma did he realize he'd been filming the wrong blonde, curly-haired grad. We had a good laugh about that later.

Spring weather anywhere can be moody; spring weather in northern Colorado is not for the faint-hearted. When my mom asked me what to expect weather-wise, I told her to bring lots of layers and prepare for anything.

I met my parents Thursday evening at the train station. "Are they still having the graduation ceremony outside?" Mom asked, pulling her blazer tighter around her as we hurried to my car. The air had a bite to it and the wind was whipping up.

"Yep, that's what they say, rain or shine. And they're predicting rain for the weekend."

Rain it did, all the next day—heavy, solid, gluttonous drops. My parents hadn't packed umbrellas, so that evening we dashed into K-Mart, soggy and dripping, then dashed back out with three golf-sized umbrellas. I pictured my family huddled on bleachers under the huge umbrellas with rivulets of water running down their backs, angry audience members yelling at them for blocking their view.

Graduation morning dawned gray and gloomy. And then I got a call on my cell phone telling me the unbeliev-able. The graduation ceremony had been cancelled.

"*What?*" I was incredulous. "But they said rain or shine." I walked over to the window and pulled back the drapes. Large flakes of snow had replaced the raindrops, burying the cars in the parking lot under thick white blankets.

Although the school had set up chairs and awnings for the ceremony, the awnings had collapsed under the weight of the heavy snow and broken several tree limbs. The field looked like a war zone, and none of the buildings on campus were large enough for the ceremony.

Neither rain, nor sleet, nor. . . I guess the Postal Service wasn't in charge of this event. Never mind the fact that my parents had just spent a wad to fly out Jordan and Gaby, my brother and sister, while pinching pennies by traveling separately by train. They'd come all this way for what was supposed to be the high point of my hard-earned scholastic training. I was their first kid to graduate from college. This wasn't how it was supposed to be!

Some kids were devastated and completely broke down. I cried a little when I first heard the news. Mom put on her best "Mom" act. "Why don't you and Tawna come over to the hotel in your caps and gowns? We'll hold our own ceremony," she suggested.

My parents snapped pictures and videotaped Tawna and me proceeding down the "grand" stair case in the hotel's front lobby while our family hummed "Pomp and Circumstance." Then they jokingly had us pose for shots by the hotel pool, lounging in our mortarboards. Suddenly, I shot up from the plastic chair—my phone was ringing. This time, the call informed me that the administration had decided to hold a modified ceremony. Grads only were invited to an abbreviated ceremony in the gym at 10:00 A.M.

We hurriedly concluded our impromptu photo shoot, snapping shots of me and Tawna holding rolled-up newspapers (since we didn't have the diplomas) under the fish sculpture mounted over the lobby fire place. "Is this what they mean by *'carpe' diem*?" Mom quipped, pointing to the fish and hinting that it was a carp (*carpe diem* being Latin for "seize the day"—a standard pronouncement on graduation days everywhere).

And so, our chaotic graduation weekend continued. Tawna and I dashed off to the school gym. Minutes later I called my parents. "I'm at the gym and they're letting some of the parents in. I'm sending my friend Liz over to get you. But Gaby and Jordan will have to stay at the hotel."

Mom and Dad arrived at the gym to find only controlled turmoil. The only place left for them to sit was above the bleachers on a catwalk, while the graduates sat kindergarten-style on mats on the floor because there was no time to set up chairs. My poor brother and sister weren't there, and there was no procession. Plus, by the time they called my name to walk up to the platform, my parents didn't have the camera ready, so they didn't get my picture. (It seems that I am simply destined not to have a photo of my own graduation.)

You know how you never remember one wedding from another after you've been to a few too many, unless it happens to be the one where the bride's veil catches on fire? This was one graduation that would stand out in our memories for sure.

If I learned anything that weekend, it's this: Stuff happens. Stuff happens a lot, actually, as I learned soon after graduation. You have a choice. You can cry, get really mad, or you can make the best of it and adapt.

My college graduation day was just like life. It's not about the pomp and ceremony. It's about the celebration, about taking life one day at a time. Stuff happens. But I graduated. It's tempting to remember only how that day failed to fulfill my expectations. But I'd prefer to relish life's unpredictability. It certainly makes things a lot more interesting.

And in the end, all we can do is *carpe diem*—seize the day. ∎

> *Yes, I am sure that neither death, nor life,*
> *nor angels, nor ruling spirits, nothing now,*
> *nothing in the future, no powers, nothing*
> *above us, nothing below us, nor anything*
> *else in the whole world will ever be able*
> *to separate us from the love of God that*
> *is in Christ Jesus our Lord.*
>
> ROMANS 8:38–39 NCV

Lifting Weights

Anyone who's ever tried to bulk up knows you won't get stronger without lifting weights. And not just any size weight will do—to increase muscle mass, you have to use weights you can lift no more than twelve times in a row, according to some fitness experts. Muscles need stress in order to grow.

In order for us to get physically stronger, our muscles have to be pushed to their limits. Likewise, in order for us to become mentally and spiritually stronger, we have to go through things that push us and stretch us. When we persevere and conquer the obstacles in front of us, we grow stronger and more able to reach for our dreams. ■

Start by doing what's necessary; then do what's possible;
and suddenly you are doing the impossible.

Francis of Assisi

God's Promises for Overcoming Challenges

So we don't look at the troubles we can see right now;
rather, we fix our gaze on things that cannot be seen.
For the things we now see will soon be gone,
but the things we cannot see will last forever.

2 CORINTHIANS 4:18 NLT

We also have joy with our troubles, because
we know that these troubles produce patience.

ROMANS 5:3

So be truly glad! There is wonderful joy ahead, even though
it is necessary for you to endure many trials for a little while.

1 PETER 1:6 NLT

Weeping may endure for a night, But joy comes in the morning.

PSALM 30:5B NKJV

I can do all things through Christ, because he gives me strength.

PHILIPPIANS 4:13

It is so good when wishes come true.

PROVERBS 13:19A

DREAMS MUST BE NOURISHED

Sometimes dreams have an incubation period. They wait, nestled in our hearts, while we finish school or save money or delay our dreams to help someone else first.

The waiting time can feel unbearable; but it's one of the most valuable times in our lives. During this time, we can nurture our dreams and let them develop and grow, becoming clearer in our minds. We can learn and collect wisdom from others' experiences. We can pray.

Downtime doesn't have to be a detriment to our dreams. Depending on how we use it, the time we spend waiting for our dreams can be one of their greatest assets.

Wherever you go,
go with all your heart.

CHINESE PROVERB

The Place to Be

MELINDA BORUM AS TOLD TO JESSICA INMAN

After several semesters with an undeclared major, it was time to officially tell my college what kind of degree I wanted. But even as I weighed the virtues of psychology and communications, I was thinking one layer above the diploma. What did I want to *do* with the rest of my life?

I wanted to graduate, for sure. But what would I do then? I wanted a deeper contentment out of life. I wanted to love every moment of whatever I did for a living.

So I got to thinking: What made me happy? What did I enjoy most?

Ever since high school, I'd loved coffee shops. I loved the frothy drinks, the mellow music, and the hours spent just talking and loving life with my friends. In college, I knew all the local coffee spots. I knew good atmosphere and good coffee—and I loved them both.

An idea began forming in my head, an idea that brought a smile to my face even as I declared Communications as my major. I wanted to start a coffeehouse of my own—the kind of place where I'd love to spend time, and where others would want to spend time too.

All through college, I collected ideas and clipped them to a bulletin board in my head—this kind of coffee, that kind of counter. It was all still just a dream, but it was becoming more detailed, more vivid.

My college graduation arrived—I finally had that diploma. Afterwards, I headed to Europe for a few amazing months. While I was there, I visited a lot of coffee shops, just like I'd always done, but this time I did so more for business than pleasure (okay, so maybe it was more like fifty-fifty on the business and pleasure).

My Europe trip ended and soon I was back home to figure out my next steps. Where did I go from here? My coffeehouse still burned in my mind, but I just wasn't sure what to do.

I had to do something. I headed for a favorite coffee spot to journal and think about the coming months. I knew I wanted to take steps toward opening my own shop; but what steps should I take? Maybe I needed to work in a coffeehouse for a while to get a feel for the business, to learn how to run a shop.

And as I sat in one of the big comfy chairs with my journal and pen in hand, I overheard the owner saying he needed someone to help out. I wasn't going to miss this opportunity. I hopped up and asked him if he would hire me. He trained me that afternoon.

During my time at Nordaggio's, I wanted to be a sponge, absorbing all the details of running a coffeehouse. And I had a ton of fun doing it.

I worked hard at Nordaggio's for about a year, and then I decided to go back to Europe since I'd loved it so much, this time for a longer stay. I spent several months in Prague, which I adored. While I was there, I found a coffee shop called the Globe which incorporated art and books with the selling of caffeinated beverages. It was such a cool little place, and I think I drew a lot of inspiration from it. And I fell more and more in love with the coffeehouse in my head.

After Prague, I spent a couple months in Spain, working as a nanny in a little tucked-away part of the country. In between my nanny duties, I had lots of time to explore the area and surf the Internet—time I spent researching coffee shops and how to start one. By the time my stay in Spain ended, I felt closer to my dream than ever.

It was Christmastime. Time to head home to the States. And as I greeted my friends and family, I knew that it was time to go for it—it was time to get serious about starting my coffeehouse.

I went back to Nordaggio's part time, intent on continuing to learn the ins and outs of the business—inventory, cash registers, all those details—with the full blessing of my boss, who knew I wanted to start my own place.

In the meantime, I got busy. I rummaged through estate sales to find the cool furniture I'd always envisioned, stashing it in my parents' garage until it could make its big debut in my shop. I went to classes at the public library on how to start a business, learning about all the legal stuff I'd always had a hard time with.

Some days, I spent hours driving around the city, scoping out good locations. I fell in love with one part of town in particular. And then one day it happened: I found a great location, and it was coming up for rent.

Getting a business loan was tricky—I was twenty-five with no collateral. But my parents, who always believed in what I was doing and to whom I am incredibly grateful, got the loan in their name, and we were able to snag the location.

I couldn't believe it—my dream was so close to coming true. Now it was time to set up shop.

I knew exactly what I wanted—soft, earthy colors on the walls, chunky mugs, offbeat furniture. I wanted the atmosphere to be mellow and organic, creating a space where people would want to linger and talk and be.

My mom is an artist, and I knew that it was sometimes hard for her to find ways to show her work— she was shy about it, and there weren't a lot of galleries in our area that would display the work of local, budding artists. And I thought about the Globe in Prague and how they offered a sort of art gallery within the dining area. So I knew I wanted my place to display the art of local talent, which would lend to the rich aesthetic experience as well as give local artists a chance to show off and sell their work.

As I began getting ready to open, all my friends and family pitched in—painting, fixing chairs, plumbing and lighting, everything. During those frenzied weeks of labor, I came to believe that when you pursue something with passion, people want to get involved, and they come alongside to help in the most amazing ways.

With their help, I got through all the hard work of setting up a business, and the following May, Shades of Brown Coffee and Art was unveiled.

Everything I'd envisioned had come to life—and the reality of owning my own shop is even better than I imagined. I love my eclectic clientele, the artists and businesspeople and students. I love the laid-back atmosphere. Most of all, I love just coming to work every day.

Business is booming, and I'm convinced that it's because I carried my dream so close to my heart and because I allowed it to grow and take the path it was meant to take. Everything about my shop is an extension of my vision and passion—I never shifted it or changed it to imitate another company's success. Sure, I've tried to make smart business and marketing moves, but the best marketing strategy I've found is to be true to my heart, which attracts just the right customers and supporters.

I think what people like about Shades of Brown is simple: It's a comfortable place to daydream and read and talk. That's what I wanted all along, and it's all because I followed my passion. ∎

*The Lord your God
has blessed you in all the work
of your hands. He has watched
over your journey through
this vast desert.*

DEUTERONOMY 2:7 NIV

Don't Go It Alone

The best things in life are meant to be shared. As you pursue your most deeply-felt dreams, sometimes it's hard to take the risk of letting someone else share the load. And yet, we all need to ask for help sometimes.

Tell someone you trust about your dream. Tell them what you hope it will be as well as your fears of what will happen along the way. Let them give you insight and advice and help you shape your dream. In the coming days, let them encourage you and look for ways to encourage them as they pursue their dreams.

Sharing a dream is the best way to keep it alive. ■

No man is an island,
entire of itself; every man is
a piece of the continent.

JOHN DONNE

Nothing is a waste
of time if you use the
experience wisely.

RODIN

The Time Between

SHARON HINCK

Shortly after my college graduation, an ugly thread slipped into my thoughts and coiled into a dark knot.

God owed me.

After all, I had prayerfully sought His direction during high school. I committed my life to serving Him and chose a Christian college and a career of church youth work. Ted and I married during our junior year. With idealism equal to my own, my husband studied toward his degree as a minister of evangelism.

The sacrifices were real. Ted loaded UPS trucks at three in the morning before classes. I juggled a variety of odd jobs—babysitting, taking in typing, doing secretarial work on campus, and choreographing at a small local theater. We squinted over rewrites of papers, refined our class projects, and volunteered at local churches. We scrimped, struggled, and invented fifty different ways to make a baked potato serve as supper.

With each sparse meal or stressful exam, we remembered we were doing this for God. He was honing and preparing us for great work for His kingdom.

At long last, we graduated. And although I wouldn't have admitted it to a soul, I figured it was time for God to show His appreciation.

Ted and I filled out forms to proclaim our availability to serve a church. In the tradition of the church body we attended, we couldn't simply go job hunting. Ministry roles were filled by a church or school offering a "call." We specified our talents and skills, our desire to work in a large city, and our hope to serve together. The paperwork went out. We kicked off our shoes, put our feet up, sank back into our old sofa, and waited for God to reveal the great destiny He had planned for us.

Only the phone never rang.

Friends scattered to various jobs. Summer dragged past and we were politely asked to leave our college apartment. We weren't students anymore. We didn't have careers. We had entered a horrible new world: the time between.

We rented half of a duplex in a rough neighborhood, our main criteria being a month-by-month lease as cheap as possible. No sense being tied into a long commitment—God had big plans for us, and we'd be getting our call soon.

I focused on my work with the Christian theater in

town. It brought in almost no income, but many dear friends. Ted and I started hosting weekly Bible studies for some of the actors who were searching for a deeper walk with God.

Ted decided to sell encyclopedias. Or try to, anyway.

Each week we called the college alumni office. "Has a call come in? Has anyone requested to meet with us?"

The answer was always the same. "Nothing yet."

Months passed. On a chilly November day, I hosted a leaf-raking party for the neighborhood children. After a puppet show with Kermit playing the role of the Good Samaritan and a shared box of gingersnaps, the kids scattered like bright maple leaves in the wind.

I trudged inside to make a pot of tea. Ted arrived soon, shoulders drooping from another unsuccessful day of extolling the benefits of leather-bound reference books. We sagged onto the sofa, cradling mugs of tea and trying to pull comfort from their warmth.

"I don't get it. We both asked God what we should do with our lives—which college to attend. We followed where He led us. And it wasn't easy. How can He ignore us like this?" I blurted out the words, then ducked my chin, ashamed of my anger.

"I don't know," Ted said quietly. We had counted on things falling into place once we graduated. The reality of daily uncertainty filled us both with a sense of failure. Everyone else we knew was busy in the "real world."

"Well, I'm not sure I like God very much right now." The words slipped out through my clenched teeth.

Beneath my irritation was bewildered pain. Had God decided He didn't want our service? That He couldn't use us? I swung between tantrums of anger and feelings of rejection. Woven through all the emotions was a constant frustration at this waste of time.

We had worked so hard to finish college and be available for God to use. Each night I crawled into bed and reminded God of the church programs I wasn't organizing, the Sunday school teachers I wasn't training, and the great work for Him that I wasn't able to accomplish—since He hadn't done His part and guided us to a church.

At last, six months after graduation, we received a call. Friends helped us load a U-haul and brave a blizzard to drive across the state to the church where we would serve.

We threw ourselves into the work for which we had trained.

But I couldn't let go of my confusion about the months of waiting. Why all that empty time? Why all those months when we did nothing of value? I laid the questions down like cards on a table, and turned them over and over. *Please help me understand*, I prayed. *It was such a painful time.*

Without words, a stream of memories flowed into my thoughts: the neighborhood children who had never heard a Bible story until we staged puppet shows for them; the theater friends who sprawled on our living room floor and dug into their walk with Christ with new zeal; the visitation skills Ted developed as he went into homes to sell encyclopedias; the casual conversations about faith issues we both had in our various odd jobs during those months; the joy of watching God provide groceries in unexpected ways when we didn't know how to stretch a dollar any further; the hours of searching, prayer, and blind stumbling.

The time between had not been an empty time. In fact, viewing it from the distance of years, I believe God accomplished more ministry through our lives in those six months of "uselessness" than in the next sixth months of official church work.

And perhaps one of His most important projects was to reveal ugly motives and expectations lurking in my own heart, and to teach me that He measures value—and time—very differently than I do.

Since graduation, I've experienced many other times between. Weeks of praying for a friend with cancer. Months of job searches. Years of struggle with weaknesses that seemed to never improve.

The time between hope and fulfillment, dream and result, or planting and harvesting still tries my patience. But I've learned. Any fragment of time God chooses to touch is full of grace and value. Even the time between. ■

But those who trust
in the LORD will find new strength.
They will soar high on wings like eagles.
They will run and not grow weary.
They will walk and not faint.

ISAIAH 40:31 NLT

Prayers to Travel By

Pursuing our dreams is a journey, sometimes a wild and unpredictable one. Some days of our journey are glorious; other days are challenging, and we wonder if we're headed the right direction. Like all adventurous journeys, we would do well to commit the pursuit of our dreams to the One who watches over our every step.

The following ancient prayer asks for protection and guidance—good things to pray for as we set out toward our dreams.

O Lord Jesus Christ our God, the true and living way, be Thou, O Master, my companion, guide, and guardian during my journey; deliver and protect me from all danger, misfortune, and temptation; that being so defended by Thy divine power, I may have a peaceful and successful journey and arrive safely at my destination. For in Thee I put my trust and hope, and to Thee, together with Thy Eternal Father, and the All-holy Spirit, I ascribe all praise, honor, and glory. . . . Amen. ∎

Only those who
will risk going too far
can possibly find out
how far one can go.

T. S. ELIOT

Most of us, swimming
against the tides of trouble
the world knows nothing about,
need only a bit of praise or
encouragement—and we
will make the goal.

JEROME FLEISHMAN

The Love Letter

ELECE HOLLIS

Boarding the bus in Lincoln, Nebraska, I was starting out on a great adventure. Janice, Carol, and Stephanie would meet me in Independence, Missouri, the jump-off town for pioneers of yesteryear and now my own jumping-off point. We were heading to the Canadian coast of British Columbia for a week of training camp, sort of a boot camp experience, before we were sent to work as summer missionaries on Indian reservations.

I trembled with excitement and nervousness as I hugged my family goodbye. Daddy huddled us together and prayed for me. Then he joked so much I knew he was anxious about sending me off. He handed me a little Brownie Box camera as he kissed me on my bangs and said, "See you in the fall, sweetie. Love you."

Mama pressed a small letter into my hand that she instructed me to read later aboard the bus. "Don't forget your seizure medicine and make sure you get enough sleep and eat right."

They were afraid for me, an epileptic, going off so far from home for the first time, and to a place where there was no hospital or doctor. If I got sick I would have to come home. Yet my parents had never held me back.

"You are the bravest of my girls," Mama told me fervently. "Despite your handicap you have always been courageous and tried hard things."

But as I hugged her goodbye, I wondered if what I was doing was beyond me. I felt a sudden surge of fear as the bus pulled out and I looked back to see Mama and Daddy, Bill, Jody, and Annie waving at me from behind the bus.

It wasn't far to Independence—three hours on the Greyhound with stops in small towns along the way. It gave me time to cry and get past the first aches of leaving home and then to argue myself past the doubts and misgivings that were just then, after all the hurrying, scurrying, and packing were done, surfacing to engulf my mind.

What was I thinking—going north to Canada to spend a whole summer on a reservation? Could I do it? I wondered what to expect. We didn't know which reservation or village we would be sent to. What would the people there be like? Would we be in danger?

All my life had been stable and according to plan. This

was a step into a dark room, a room full of unknowns, where there might be holes in the floor, enemies afoot, dangers lurking.

I hoped, above all, that I wouldn't get sick so that the other girls would have to take care of me. I hoped to prove my capabilities since it was my dream to serve on a foreign mission field someday.

My mind still swirling with all the what-ifs and maybes, I took out my letter and read it. And as I did, courage welled up in my heart and tears in my eyes. With such a mother I didn't have to worry. Who could fail with a mom who knew the perfect words to ease a young woman's mind?

The girls were waiting and we loaded up in Janice's car and headed west. We drove through Nebraska and Wyoming, up and across Montana and the panhandle of Idaho, winding our way through Washington until we reached the Canadian border, where we entered British Columbia and headed for the coast to ferry over to Vancouver Island.

The letter was put away carefully, but not forgotten, amongst all the new sights and sounds. I didn't have a chance to feel homesick or frightened until at the end of the training, two of us were assigned to a small reservation in Washington State. The local school teacher had left for the summer and loaned us her house. We set to work, teaching sports and hand-crafts along with leading Bible classes, church services, and children's Bible club.

The children were happy to have us and the rainforest and North Pacific beaches were beautiful and inspiring. But I lost my momentum when Stephanie injured her eye and had to go home where she could get the medical care she needed. I sent her off with a brave face, and then I returned to the reservation, facing the summer's work alone and afraid. Fear I had tucked way down deep inside came sprouting up. I couldn't call home. Mail came, but not often and not today.

I rummaged in my duffel bag for the letter. I read it until I could hear Mom's voice, imagine Dad's arm around me, and feel my family and Jesus near.

The letter that I read over and over and which sustained me through the rest of that tough summer and many seasons of my life since, read simply: "Your mama loves you! Your daddy loves you! Your grandmother loves you! Your aunts love you! Your uncle loves you! Your friends love you! Your brothers love you! Your sisters love you! And Jesus loves you! You are *very* loved!"

Those were the words. They were just what I needed to battle loneliness and fear as I faced the unknown. I carried my family's love with me on my journey that summer, and it in turn carried me and lifted me closer to my dreams. ∎

Your love has given me great
joy and encouragement.

PHILEMON 1:7A NIV

God's Promises
for Nurturing Dreams

*Take delight in the LORD, and
he will give you your heart's desires.*

PSALM 37:4 NLT

*This is what the Lord, who saves you,
the Holy One of Israel, says: "I am
the Lord your God, who teaches you
to do what is good, who leads you
in the way you should go."*

ISAIAH 48:17

*But if any of you needs wisdom, you should
ask God for it. He is generous and enjoys giving
to all people, so he will give you wisdom.*

JAMES 1:5

*Trust the Lord with all your heart, and
don't depend on your own understanding.
Remember the Lord in all you do,
and he will give you success.*

PROVERBS 3:5–6

*You have begun to live the new life,
in which you are being made new and are
becoming like the One who made you.*

COLOSSIANS 3:10A

So I do not run without a goal.
I fight like a boxer who is hitting
something—not just the air.

1 Corinthians 9:26

DREAMS REQUIRE WORK

~~~~~

Besides obstacles and challenges, the other thing all dreams have in common is that they absolutely will not get off the ground without work. It takes commitment and effort and energy to turn a dream into a reality.

The good news is that even though there will be days when we don't want to do the work, if our dream is really worthwhile, the work itself becomes something we relish. Following our dreams isn't only about the destination; it's about the journey. And when we commit ourselves to the work of making our dreams come true, we're assured that both the journey and the destination will be a joy.

Hard work spotlights
the character of people:
some turn up their sleeves,
some turn up their
noses, and some don't
turn up at all.

SAM EWING

Mr. Goodwrench

GLENN A. HASCALL

Legs were sticking out from underneath the old pickup I was helping to overhaul. Those legs belonged to my dad.

He had always been one to tinker. If something was broken or not working quite right, he would hop right into the midst of the situation until he came up with an answer. Me? Well, I was content to let him. I would help out if he told me what to do, but frankly I was much more comfortable letting other people handle the bulk of the repair work.

I changed the oil in my vehicles for years, but with the advent of the chain quick-lube places, I pretty much swore off changing oil. In fact, I haven't done so in years, and I don't even really feel all that guilty about it. But I do remember working with my dad. He would be under a vehicle with some handheld tool or another, trying to loosen or tighten some bolt. It invariably would come loose just as he was applying the most elbow grease, thrusting his hand at warp speed directly into some metal component placed by the manufacturer at the perfect angle to wrench skin from his knuckles or fingers.

This was often followed by a spirited rendition of the Hallelujah Chorus.

Even today, every time I see him I can always tell when he's been doing some mechanic work. The bandages or healing skin give him away.

My dad taught me more than just how to change oil, though. He also taught me the value of a good work ethic. I started working when I was fourteen. By the time my senior year of high school rolled around, I had worked at several different jobs and was the proud owner of a half-ton pickup truck. I had secured the loan under my own name and was looking toward the future.

But soon I decided that I had a problem: I didn't want to work. I was a senior and I wanted to participate in the school musical. In order to do that, I had to have plenty of free time.

I tried out and was surprised when I landed the lead in *Oklahoma*. Lots of singing and gunplay and action—a dream come true. But what was I supposed to do about my job and the payment on my pickup?

So I decided to talk with Dad about it, and he came up with a solution. It was one of those good news/bad news situations. The good news: I could trade my pickup straight across for a car and I would no longer have any payments—the car would be mine free and clear, and I could stop working. Bad news: The car was about the ugliest thing I had ever seen.

I took the car.

A friend of mine repainted it for me, spiffing it up nicely, and I could finally participate in the musical without having a job to worry about.

It wasn't long after the curtain closed, though, that I came to the conclusion that employment had its benefits. It had not occurred to eighteen-year-old me that it takes more than wishing and hoping to fill the tank of an eight cylinder vehicle and pay for the insurance necessary to operate the vehicle, let alone the oil and filter that needed changing and the tires that needed replacing. By Christmas I would rejoin the workforce.

That year, I took away some pretty wonderful memories of the hard work it took to put a musical together, memories of my dad who helped make that possible, and memories of driving the ugly car I came to love. And since that time, so many things in my life have come to me by the sweat of my brow—or the skin of my knuckles. Simply put, there is reward in a job well done.

My dad taught me how to change my oil. He also taught me to work, and work well. ∎

Whatever you do, do well.

ECCLESIASTES 9:10A NLT

Be strong!

It matters not how deep intrenched the wrong,
How hard the battle goes, the day how long;
Faint not—fight on! To-morrow comes the song.

FROM "BE STRONG" BY MALTBIE DAVENPORT BABCOCK

Let us not become weary in doing good,
for at the proper time we will reap
a harvest if we do not give up.

GALATIANS 6:9 NIV

All that stands
between the graduate
and the top of the
ladder is the ladder.

AUTHOR UNKNOWN

You Da Man

NANETTE THORSEN-SNIPES

While I desperately wanted my oldest son to go to college, I knew that with three other mouths to feed and my family's mounting bills, it would have to wait. I was more than proud, however, as he walked down the aisle and accepted his high school diploma. I just didn't know how he'd ever be able to get further than a waiter at a four-star restaurant. But he did.

Over sandwiches and iced tea years later, I asked David how he became so successful since he and his younger brother and I had done without so many things over the years. David, now the general manager of a prominent Atlanta hotel and successful beyond his imagination, looked thoughtful for a moment. And then as we munched on chips, he began to relate a story I'd never heard.

"Several years ago," he started, "I presented an orientation where I sat across from six of my newest employees. It was an informal orientation—we were just hanging out, getting to know people and letting them get to know me and the hotel."

After a greeting and the usual statement of "We're glad you're with us and part of the team," David opened the floor for questions.

"How did you get to where you are? I mean, how did you do it?" a housekeeper sitting in the back asked.

"Actually," he answered, "it started when I was seven years old. My mother and father divorced and Mom moved into an apartment. She sat me down one day and said, 'David, you're the man of the family now, and you have to come home from school, put your things up, and go next door to the neighbor's. You have to be responsible, young man.'"

David smiled at the group. "I stepped up to that responsibility and learned how to get off the bus by myself and let myself in the apartment. Then, I went next door just as Mom said. I think I started learning responsibility then.

"Later, when I was fifteen, Mom kind of guided me into my first part-time job. It was one she thought suited my personality, working as a busboy cleaning tables in a four-star restaurant dining room. I liked the restaurant business immediately, and I really wanted to succeed, so I paid attention to people who made it to the top.

"We had a much-admired waiter team called George

and Rick who made a lot of tips as waiters. I also noticed that their personal busboy made more tips than anyone else. So my goal became to work with George and Rick by being the very best busboy.

"I started really working hard at my bussing job. Soon, I became the quickest and most efficient of all the busboys. Then I started carrying my own crumber, which sweeps a table of crumbs. I learned how to efficiently change a tablecloth without ever showing the table. Soon, George and Rick noticed my attention to detail and my desire to improve. They asked me to become their busboy.

"Since Rick, who was the back waiter, didn't like making Caesar salads tableside, I offered to take over. I learned how to make the best Caesar salads ever. Then I learned how to make desserts and talk in front of people. And so when Rick retired, George chose me to be the new back waiter.

"Then," said David to the spellbound group of new employees, "I became the best back waiter there was. I had to conquer the skill of delivering food. The bottom line was that I came into work every day and took responsibility by doing the absolute best I could.

"Over time, I worked my way into doing presenta tions with George. By doing more and more of George's job, I was rewarded by splitting George's gratuity fifty-fifty instead of receiving the usual fifteen percent.

"When George was promoted to maitre d', I took his place and determined to be the best front waiter the restaurant had, learning more about food, drink, and decor.

"Step by step, I moved up the line, achieving almost everything I set my mind to. From waiter to restaurant manager to marketing manager, nothing was impossible. I simply did the best I could in each position."

As I listened to my son talk, I felt proud realizing that even as David took on more and more "important" roles, he kept working hard and humbly, and he kept looking out for his fellow workers. David said he made an effort to eat lunch with the chef, asking how his day went. I was amazed how my son found the time to talk one-on-one with the doorman. And when he said he folded clothes with the housekeeping team while asking about their jobs, I almost clapped.

David's story was winding down. A woman in the employee meeting squirmed in her chair and timidly raised her hand, and David called on her. "Could I ask you a silly question?" she asked.

"Sure."

"I noticed your cufflinks. Those aren't your initials, are they?" she asked.

David smiled as he recalled his last day at his former job. "I'm glad you asked. No, those aren't my initials.

"When I left my last position, my assistant and employees gave me a light blue box from Tiffany's. I couldn't imagine what was in the box, but knowing my employees' sense of humor, I was prepared for anything.

"When I opened it, there were these silver cufflinks with the initials YDM. I knew I'd truly succeeded when all my employees shouted, 'David, you da man!'

"I guess I better explain," he said. "Soon after I started work with their hotel, my employees started saying, 'You da man,' every time they saw me. And I'd say, 'No, you da man!'

"And every time one of my employees did something outstanding like bringing hot towels and a bottle of cold water for customers who'd been out running, I'd encourage them by saying, 'You da man!'"

As we prepared to leave our lunch meeting, I had a newfound respect for my son. I hugged him and whispered in his ear, "David, you da man!"

Maybe David didn't make it to college, but he certainly graduated from the school of life, landing at the top of his profession. He couldn't have done it without working hard and giving his best to even the most humble jobs. But by doing his best and committing the rest to God, he soared to new heights. ■

Do your work with enthusiasm.
Work as if you were serving
the Lord, not as if you were serving
only men and women.

EPHESIANS 6:7

Go for the Gold

Following our dreams takes work—and time.

- Top marathon runners often put in around 100 miles a week. Average runners need to train for at least twenty-six weeks to be ready for a marathon.
- Most elite swimmers train three to five hours a day, six days a week.
- Most NFL teams practice eight hours a day.
- Members of the New York Philharmonic rehearse about twenty hours a week, on top of one to three hours a day of individual practice.

If you've got long stretches of work ahead of you in order to achieve your dream, remember that the work is necessary—and that your efforts will pay off.

All the so-called "secrets of success"
will not work unless you do.

Author Unknown

God's Promises for Perseverance

Keep on asking, and you will receive what you ask for.
Keep on seeking, and you will find. Keep on knocking,
and the door will be opened to you.

MATTHEW 7:7 NLT

Wealth gained by dishonesty will be diminished,
But he who gathers by labor will increase.

PROVERBS 13:11 NKJV

You must hold on, so you can do what
God wants and receive what he has promised.

HEBREWS 10:36

Lord our God, treat us well. Give us success
in what we do; yes, give us success in what we do.

PSALM 90:17

*"I say this because
I know what I am planning
for you," says the Lord. "I have
good plans for you, not plans
to hurt you. I will give you
hope and a good future."*

JEREMIAH 29:11

DREAMS DETERMINE OUR TOMORROWS

~~~~~~~~~~~~~~~~~~~~~~~~

One of the best things about dreams is the light they shed on the future. When we actively follow our dreams, we may not know exactly what the days ahead will bring, but we know that we're moving in the direction we want to. And we know that the future may very well bring us things more wonderful than our highest expectations.

When we follow our dreams, they carry us to wonderful places and wonderful days.

We all have dreams.
But in order to make
dreams come into reality,
it takes an awful lot of
determination, dedication,
self-discipline, and effort.

JESSE OWENS

A Teacher at Last

EUGENE EDWARDS AS TOLD TO GLORIA CASSITY STARGEL

It was now or never.

At my shop that wintry afternoon, I pulled on my black overcoat and stepped outside. With my hand on the doorknob, I paused. After thirty years in the plumbing business, it was time to follow my heart. I shut the door for the last time and hung up a sign: "Gone out of business."

Then, feeling a little like David going out to fight Goliath with only a slingshot, I climbed into my car and at age fifty turned all thoughts toward my lifelong dream of being a schoolteacher. *Lord, You've brought me this far*, I pleaded silently, *please don't leave me now or I'll fail for sure.*

The teacher who taught me life lessons never would have called himself a teacher.

Mr. Roy was my mentor, my role model. He would talk to me and ask me questions—treat me like I was somebody.

I was about six. There was a little family-run store in our neighborhood, and Mr. Roy and some other old-timers were usually there, propped on upside-down nail kegs, playing a round of checkers and swapping yarns. I'd sidle up to the checkerboard to "help out" Mr. Roy with his game.

And it was there, at Mr. Roy's elbow, that many of my values and certainly my life's goal were formed. Not that my parents didn't teach me things. They did. But as there were seventeen of us children at home, individual attention was hard to come by.

"Eugene," Mr. Roy said one day, "what do you want to be when you grow up?"

"A teacher," I fairly blurted out. Then added with a self-conscious swagger, "That's what I want to be—a schoolteacher."

In a tone which left no room for doubt Mr. Roy responded, "Then be one!"

Mr. Roy could see the pitfalls ahead, however. "Eugene," he said, dead serious as he wrapped one bony arm around my equally thin shoulders, "there will be times when folks will say, 'You can't do that.' Just take it in stride and set out to prove them wrong."

With those conversations locked tight in my memory, my dream was set in my heart like stone. But during my junior year of high school, my mom passed away. I knew then that my going to college and becoming a teacher was out of the question. Dad needed me to help him care for the younger children. So I took up a trade instead—plumbing.

As I did, I recalled another of Mr. Roy's sayings. "Whatever you become," he'd said, "whether you're a ditch-digger or a schoolteacher, you be the best you can be. That's all the good Lord asks of us."

That's exactly what I tried to do for thirty years. I learned all I could and practiced what I believed—do it right the first time and you don't have to go back. Eventually I had my own business. In the early years I even managed to take a college course here and there, but abandoned that effort when my plumbing work became too demanding. All the while, though, buried deep in the heart, my dream of someday being a teacher pulsed on.

The day came, though, when my long-dreamed dream no longer would be denied. Knowing how much I loved kids and seeing how much they needed positive role models, I closed my shop. I knew I had to start taking steps to fulfilling my dream.

Four days later, I started work at Hendrix Drive Elementary School—not as a teacher, but as a custodian.

I figured the job would be a good way to get a feel for the school environment, to test the waters, so to speak. It was a beginning.

Right away, I hit it off with the students. Soon they knew me by name, and the principal even let me read to some of the lower grades.

I met so many kids—like my young friend Johnny— who had come from broken homes, being raised by their single mom or by a grandmother. They were hungry for a positive male role model, someone who would show genuine interest in them, show them they are loved. They desperately need a Mr. Roy in their lives. I wanted to be that one.

I had time to do a lot of thinking and praying while I polished those floors. Sometimes I thought I didn't need to become a teacher—I was doing a pretty good job reaching out to kids as a custodian. Even Principal Soper called me "an excellent role model."

But then one day I heard God speak to me, and I knew that He wanted me to go as far as I could in helping students. I could hear Mr. Roy saying, "Never settle for second best, Eugene. Whatever you become, you be the best you can be."

So one night I ventured to the family, "Looks like I'm going to have to go to college after all." As they rallied behind me, I signed up for night and weekend classes at the Norcross branch of Brenau University.

Still working forty hours a week at the school, before long I found myself studying many nights until one or two in the morning, only to get up at 5:30 in order to be at work by 6:30. Often, while cleaning those floors, I carried on a running dialogue with Jesus. "Lord, I'm bone weary. Remind me again that this is something You want me to do. 'Cause if it's just my wanting it, I'm about ready to quit."

In answer, I believe God sent Johnny back to me. Johnny had graduated from our middle school the year before; now he came by to visit and found me about to replace a fluorescent bulb in a hallway fixture. "Johnny, I am so glad to see you!" I said, giving him a big bear hug. "How're you doing, son?"

"Fine, sir," he replied. "Mr. Edwards," he went on, "I want to thank you for the time you spent with me here, for caring about me. I never would have made it through sixth grade if it hadn't been for you."

"Johnny, I am so proud of you," I responded, stepping off the ladder to look him in the eye. "And you're going to finish high school, aren't you?"

"Yes, sir," he said, his face breaking into a huge smile, "I'm even going to college, Mr. Edwards—like you!"

I almost cried to think I had influenced him that much. I determined then and there to stick it out with my studies. Johnny was counting on me, as would other Johnnys yet to come.

And now it's early morning on a spring day, a day that will go down in history, or at least my history—it's graduation day. I'm driving fifty miles to Gainesville for rehearsal, and my family will follow for the ceremony. On the seat beside me is my black robe and mortarboard with tassel, and out loud I keep saying, "Praise You, Jesus! Thank You, Jesus."

The rain has eased up by the time I park. I sit in the car several minutes, basking in the glow. I can't deny it. Tears of happiness threaten to run off down my cheeks.

At the ceremony, I am almost overcome with emotion. As the music swells, the processional begins with Brenau's president and faculty in full academic regalia looking impressive indeed. When my turn comes, I somehow get up onto the stage to receive my diploma but I never feel my feet touch the floor.

I float back to my seat, beaming like a lit-up Christmas tree, clutching the tangible evidence of a long-dreamed dream come true: a square of parchment with those all-important words, Bachelor of Science Degree in Middle Grades Education.

It just goes to show, if you dream long enough—and work hard enough—the good Lord will help make your dream come true.

I'm a teacher at last!

Mr. Roy would be proud. ■

Wishes that come true are like
eating fruit from the tree of life.

PROVERBS 13:12B

Good Days Ahead

What do you want your life to look like in the coming years? Writing down your goals for the next month, year, and five or ten years will help solidify them in your mind and give your days a sense of purpose.

Once you've written your list, pray over it, committing your future to your Father. The psalmist wrote, "Commit your way to the Lord; trust in him and he will do this: He will make your righteousness shine like the dawn, the justice of your cause like the noonday sun" (Psalm 37:5–6). When we dream big and listen for God's will, we're assured of a bright future. ■

Always continue to fear the LORD.
You will be rewarded for this;
your hope will not be disappointed.
PROVERBS 23:17A–18 NLT

Faith for Tomorrow

THOMAS CURTIS CLARK

"Tomorrow, friend, will be another day,"
A seer wise of old was wont to say
To him who came at eventide, in grief,
Because the day had borne no fruitful sheaf.

O Lord of Life, that each of us might learn
From vain todays and yesterdays to turn,
To face the future with a hope newborn
That what we hope for cometh with the morn! ■

*Three grand essentials to happiness
in this life are something to do, something
to love, and something to hope for.*

JOSEPH ADDISON

It is a mistake
to look too far ahead.
Only one link in the
chain of destiny may be
handled at a time.

SIR WINSTON CHURCHILL

Lights

JESSICA INMAN

I press the last push-pin into the wall. I am daringly/
foolishly perched on my toes on my swiveling desk chair,
arranging some white Christmas lights into a lattice
formation above my closet door. Some events in my life in
the last few months—my birthday and college graduation,
among other things—have precipitated several greeting
cards from special people, and I want to display them in
my room in some creative fashion.

I hop back on the chair after retrieving the cards, and
begin sliding them between the lights and the wall; some
of them I leave open to reveal the words of kindness and
encouragement scrawled on the inside. When I'm done,
the space of wall above my closet is a visual patchwork—
little squares of handwriting, an ice cream cone, a dog with
a hologram bone above his sleepy head.

I plug in the lights, rendering the cards illumined and
sparkly. I sigh. Is there something wrong with me? Because
I don't know exactly what I should do next with my life,
and I think that I am supposed to.

I graduated from college in May with absolutely
no idea what I was going to do on Monday. With a
hodgepodge of skills and a sense of passion sketchy at best,
I tried out many different ideas throughout the summer.
I felt vaguely pulled toward urban relief work, youth
ministry, and writing in some capacity or another, but
I didn't really know how to move forward or decipher a
sense of "call" amid those thoughts and desires.

Thus, the job hunt was rather complicated. I developed a
résumé, applied at a student missions organization, and made
some contacts within my denomination with a budding inner-
city church in another part of the state. Meanwhile, I kept my
comfy position as a youth pastor's secretary.

I interviewed at the inner-city church and eventually
landed an administrative assistant position with them. I
informed my boss that I would be leaving after September.
But I was also seeking counsel with an urban ministry
leader in my own city, who warned me that if I plunged
into urban work without clarity about God's purpose
in my life, the road ahead would be hard and possibly
disastrous. I decided to heed that warning, along with the
war in my stomach over the whole affair. I declined the
position only a few days before I was scheduled to move.

My last day as youth group secretary just happened to be the day after the publication of my first article. My boss, Doug, insisted that he take me to lunch that day; I consented. I walked into the restaurant and thought, "Wow, the whole church office staff decided to come to lunch at the same restaurant Doug picked today," not realizing this was my going away/congratulations party.

I got a card signed by the staff, a few very sweet gifts, some kudos on my article, and a bowl of baked potato soup. This was Friday; on Monday, I would have no job.

I told Doug I'd help him out a little bit during the interim—they hadn't found my replacement yet, and I was happy to help him with the things that drive him the craziest while I looked for something with a few more hours a week. In the end, I found myself without much direction, and ended up rejoining the staff at the church permanently to pay bills while I write and otherwise try to make money however I can. As much as the office staff had wished me well when I "left," they welcomed me back equally warmly. I baked cookies and left them in the workroom with a card that said, "I love you people."

I look again at the cards now spread on my wall and read some of the inscriptions. Gloria writes on my goodbye card, "What a beautiful young woman of God you are—both inside and out! I am really going to miss you!" On my birthday card, Mollie writes, "Your metamorphosis into adulthood has been a joy to behold." And then I read Bryan's card. I get a little misty reading what he—someone I have admired and sometimes felt like I have failed— admires about me.

I stand under the lights and think to myself, *these people really seem to love me*. And I don't think I understand that.

I can tolerate lack of direction in other people. It makes perfect sense to me that other people my age may struggle a little in figuring out what they were created to do the first year or two after college. But in myself, I don't suffer aimlessness gladly. And so I am thoroughly perplexed by these short messages of love from my coworkers.

Perplexed, but grateful. And deeply conscious of the security God has given me through these people. Feeling their love, I can press on, maybe making a couple of fairly alarming mistakes, but knowing that things will turn out, that God has gifted me in certain ways and wants to guide me. There is an interesting hope in feeling loved and appreciated, and knowing that this love comes ultimately from someone who directs my every step.

It's getting late. I guess I should get to bed. After all, who knows what tomorrow will bring, what shy steps God will beckon me to take toward the future? I unplug the Christmas lights, hesitate a moment, then plug them back in. I may leave them on all night. ■

Trust in the LORD with all your heart
and lean not on your own understanding;
in all your ways acknowledge him, and
he will make your paths straight.

PROVERBS 3:5–6 NIV

And in today already
walks tomorrow.

SAMUEL TAYLOR COLERIDGE

Teach us to realize the brevity of life, so that
we may grow in wisdom. . . . Satisfy us
each morning with your unfailing love, so
we may sing for joy to the end of our lives.

PSALM 90:12, 14 NLT

God's Promises
for Bright Tomorrows

Jesus Christ is the same yesterday, today, and forever.

HEBREWS 13:8

The Lord will guard you as you
come and go, both now and forever.

PSALM 121:8A

The Lord says, "I will make you wise and show you
where to go. I will guide you and watch over you."

PSALM 32:8

He satisfies me with good things
and makes me young again, like the eagle.

PSALM 103:5

There is surely a future hope for you,
and your hope will not be cut off.

PROVERBS 23:18 NIV

The Lord says, "Forget what happened before, and do not think about the past. Look at the new thing I am going to do. It is already happening. Don't you see it? I will make a road in the desert and rivers in the dry land."

ISAIAH 43:18–19

DREAMS WILL GROW AND CHANGE

We are not the same people we will be five years from now, or even five minutes from now. Our circumstances and surroundings are constantly changing us and shaping us.

So it's important that we make our choices carefully, prayerfully considering how we live our lives to ensure that we're growing in a positive direction. And in God's faithfulness, He promises to continue working on us and making us more like Him.

And as we grow and change, our dreams will grow too, becoming richer and more exciting and more fitting to the people we've come to be.

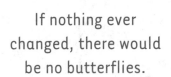

If nothing ever
changed, there would
be no butterflies.

AUTHOR UNKNOWN

Major Disappointment

KATE FREZON AS TOLD TO PEGGY FREZON

Ever since I held my grandfather's old slide rule, I've always loved numbers. When other kids were playing with Barbie dolls and riding their bikes, I was counting things. I'd line up my Beanie Babies across my bedroom floor, arrange them by color, and count them. I'd count the cracks in the sidewalk. I once gave my mother a handmade birthday card with the touching sentiment "2 + 3 = 5." So it was only natural that I dreamed of becoming a mathematician.

On the day of my high school graduation, I sat in my seat only half listening to the speeches booming from the stage as I reflected on my mathematically-inclined childhood. I thought back as far as I could remember, to nursery school when I was a rosy-cheeked, curly-haired little girl, nervous about being left alone. My mom dropped me off and asked, "Okay, how long before I come pick you up again?"

I looked at the big silver clock on the wall. "Three hours and twelve minutes." I understood that the hands on the clock counted the hours and minutes, the same way I liked to count. Before kindergarten I'd mastered addition and subtraction, as well as multiplication and division. I don't know how. I didn't study. I wasn't drilled. I just understood numbers. It seemed that math would be my destiny.

Years later, I sat in class as a freshman at Cornell University. I loved Cornell, and was thrilled to be accepted as a math major. The only drawback was the annoying liberal arts classes I was required to take. What use did I have for history, English, and philosophy when all I wanted to do was math?

I did have a few math classes, though. Confidently, I'd enrolled in an upper level calculus course. Why not? Calculus in high school had been a breeze. I also signed up for Statistics for Engineers. A few years before, I'd taken a statistics course at the local university and received an A. This shouldn't be much different, right?

But the classes were much more difficult than I'd expected. I had to work really hard to maintain decent grades. And surprisingly, the classes weren't all that fun. I was conflicted. Wasn't math the course that God had intended for me? Why else had He given me these skills?

Even more surprisingly, the required liberal arts courses I'd scoffed at so much in the beginning proved to be some of the most interesting and compelling subjects in my course load. I actually enjoyed in-depth studies about linguistics, ancient cultures, and women in literature.

Suddenly I realized that there was a whole world of studies out there in addition to mathematics. And some of it was a lot more interesting.

"You know, I'm not so sure about being a math major anymore," I said to my friend Josh one day.

"Well, think about what kind of job you might want after college," he replied. "What do you have fun doing?"

I thought about my work-study job in the University Performing Arts Center and my experiences helping out behind the scenes in productions. That was definitely fun. "I'm going to switch majors," I told my parents the next day. "I'm going to be a theater major!"

The idea didn't go over so well. "But, honey, you're not an actress," my mom said. "And there aren't so many job openings for stage crew, are there?"

"How will you pay back all those college loans?" asked my dad.

I had to admit, it wasn't a totally practical idea. I just thought it would be fun. So I went to classes and did some more thinking. One day I was in my computer science class.

I had already ruled out computer science as a major; it was too "techie." But at the time we were studying Web pages and the Internet, and I found the chapter really exciting.

This was something I could do. I went to my advisor and researched some more. That's when I came up with the perfect major: information science. It was a combination of math and science, but also involved graphics, psychology, and human interaction. Right then and there I changed my major and began a fascinating course of study learning how to improve the way people and companies use computers.

Now, as I am about to graduate from college, I am glad I was forced to take a wide variety of classes. If not, I'd never be exposed to so many new ideas. I didn't know it then, but those dreaded liberal arts courses helped me discover an exciting new possibility. I still love numbers—and I still love to count things—but I also know something else I love: I love that I can count on God to lead me in new and unexpected ways. ■

*He makes me to lie down
in green pastures; He leads me
beside the still waters. He restores
my soul; He leads me in the
paths of righteousness
for His name's sake.*

PSALM 23:2–3 NKJV

You Never Know

History is full of career changes. Lots of people start out on one path, then switch to another. Consider these examples—

- Denzel Washington earned a college degree in journalism before he turned to acting.
- Jeffrey Bezos, founder of Web retail giant Amazon.com, planned to study physics in college before deciding to pursue a career in computers.
- Thomas Edison sold fruit and vegetables and worked as a telegraph operator before creating his first official invention, an electronic vote-counting machine.

- Actor Liam Neeson of *Star Wars* and *Schindler's List* fame reportedly originally wanted to be a butcher. Before landing his first theater role, he studied to be a teacher and was a youth heavyweight boxing champion.

Feel free to try new things and explore the world around you! You never know what new dreams God may place in your heart. ■

Continuity gives us roots;
change gives us branches,
letting us stretch and grow
and reach new heights.

PAULINE R. KEZER

If anyone belongs to Christ,
there is a new creation.
The old things have gone;
everything is made new!

2 CORINTHIANS 5:17

Though no one
can go back and make
a brand new start,
anyone can start
from now and make
a brand new ending.

AUTHOR UNKNOWN

The world needs
dreamers and the
world needs doers.
But above all, the world
needs dreamers who do.

SARAH BAN BREATHNACH

When Visions Grow

It started simple.

Sam was an entrepreneur from the beginning—he put himself through college with newspaper routes, adding routes and hiring helpers until he was earning up to $4,000 a year. After his stint in the military was done, all he wanted was to open a store. It wasn't a grandiose vision. He just wanted to own his own store and provide an enjoyable shopping experience.

And so he opened a variety store in Newport, Arkansas. It was successful—very successful. Customers and analysts alike would later attribute the success of that store to Sam's values, his love for hard work, his cheerfulness and optimism, and his talent for making people feel connected and important.

In three years, the store nearly tripled its sales. Unfortunately, the lease was not renewed, and Sam lost his store.

He was down, but not out. He'd learned a lot about the business and about trends in retail, and he had new dreams and visions, bigger ones. He opened another store in Bentonville, Arkansas. This store was something brand new: It was only the third self-service variety store in the nation, and the first in the state. Previously, general stores were arranged so that the clerk brought the merchandise to the customer; in this new way of constructing stores, customers could examine the merchandise on store shelves before bringing them to the clerk to purchase.

Sam's vision expanded—more stores, offering the customer the lowest price and highest quality possible. His stores multiplied until he and his brother were running a chain of fifteen stores. Along the way, his vision of how to do business began to solidify. He'd discovered that by offering lower prices, he could sell a higher volume and make a larger profit than by charging as much as he could get away with. He also knew that his customers wanted more variety, which meant larger stores, which meant defying conventional wisdom when it came to running variety stores.

He asked his merchandiser for lower prices so that he could fulfill this vision. When they declined, he knew it was time to set out on his own.

So he and his wife opened the very first Wal-Mart store in Rogers, Arkansas, fronting 95% of the money themselves.

From there, things just got bigger. Within ten years, the number of stores had doubled, and they were bringing in over $30 million a year. Ten years after that, they broke the $1 billion mark. And today, Wal-Mart sales have climbed to over $250 billion in revenue, and the number of stores has climbed to around five thousand.

As the sales and number of stores have grew, so did Sam Walton's vision. He saw the potential for different kinds of stores, price clubs and superstores. He also saw how his company could use technology: Wal-Mart invented and was the first to implement an electronic data-sharing system between stores and their suppliers, resulting in more efficient stocking and shipping.

Even with all these changes, though—even though Sam's original vision to own his own store changed and shifted and became enlarged over the course of many years—his basic goal had stayed the same: to provide his customers with the things they needed.

Sometimes when a vision changes, it becomes smaller—and that's okay, because a smaller vision is what best serves the needs of others. But sometimes a vision changes for the bigger, and with consistency and persistence on our part, before long it's bigger than our wildest dreams. It's all a matter of our willingness to follow our dreams wherever they go and wherever they best serve others.

Big or small, a vision fulfilled meets a need in the world—and creates contentment in our hearts.

Listen now to my voice;
I will give you counsel,
and God will be with you.
Exodus 18:19 NKJV

God's Promises for Growing Dreams

God is working in you to help you want
to do and be able to do what pleases him.

PHILIPPIANS 2:13

God has said, "I will never leave you; I will never forget you."

HEBREWS 13:5B

Trust the Lord with all your heart, and don't
depend on your own understanding. Remember
the Lord in all you do, and he will give you success.

PROVERBS 3:5–6

Now, may the God of peace—who brought up from
the dead our Lord Jesus, the great Shepherd of the sheep,
and ratified an eternal covenant with his blood.

HEBREWS 13:20A NLT

Because you were loyal with small things,
I will let you care for much greater things.

MATTHEW 25:21B

ACKNOWLEDGMENTS

"Carpe Diem" © Teena M. Stewart. Used by permission. All rights reserved.

"A Dream Fulfilled" © Jan Madden. Used by permission. All rights reserved.

"Follow Your Heart" © Margaret Lang. Used by permission. All rights reserved.

"Lights" © Jessica Inman. Used by permission. All rights reserved.

"The Love Letter" © Elece Hollis. Used by permission. All rights reserved.

"Major Disappointment" © Peggy Frezon. Used by permission. All rights reserved.

"More Than a Grasshopper" © Margaret Lang. Used by permission. All rights reserved.

"Mr. Goodwrench" © Glenn A. Hascall. Used by permission. All rights reserved.

"The Place to Be" © Jessica Inman. Used by permission. All rights reserved.

"Sarah's Tea Table" © Elece Hollis. Used by permission. All rights reserved.

"Smiley" © Karen Majoris Garrison. Used by permission. All rights reserved.

"Take a Risk" © Shane Werlinger. Used by permission. All rights reserved.

"A Teacher at Last" © Gloria Cassity Stargel. Used by permission. All rights reserved.

"The Time Between" © Sharon Hinck. Used by permission. All rights reserved.

"When Visions Grow" © Jessica Inman. Used by permission. All rights reserved.

"Wildflowers" © Kitty Chappell. Used by permission. All rights reserved.

"You Da Man" © Nanette Thorsen-Snipes. Used by permission. All rights reserved.